The Elf on the Shelf's
Night Before Christmas

by Chanda A. Bell

The LumiStella Company
www.lumistella.com

To Clement C. Moore and the creativity he inspires, as well as
Kendyl and Taylor – may Christmas Eve always be magical.
With special thanks to Frank Huff for his service and
commitment to the work of Santa's North Pole.
—CAB

CCA and B, LLC d/b/a The Lumistella Company
3350 Riverwood Parkway SE, Suite 300
Atlanta, GA 30339 USA - É.-U. - EE.UU.

www.elfontheshelf.com

13 12 11 10 9 8 7 6 5 4

Library of Congress Cataloging-in-Publication Data

Bell, Chanda A.

    The Elf on the Shelf's Night Before Christmas / written by Chanda A. Bell

        p. cm.

Summary: Follow along on this playful adventure in a classic retold by one of Santa's Scout Elves. This whimsical
take on "The Night Before Christmas" features a Scout Elf and his Elf Pets pals caught in Christmas Eve chaos,
while Santa keeps the season merry with a touch of Christmas Magic.
–Provided by Publisher

ISBN-13: 978-0-9600665-7-5

PRINTED AND BOUND IN CHINA / IMPRIMÉ ET RELIÉ EN CHINE / IMPRESO Y ENCUADERNADO EN CHINA

The Elf on the Shelf's
Night Before Christmas

'Twas the Night before Christmas,
and all through the house,
a few creatures stirred
but not one was a mouse.
The stockings were hung
by the chimney with care,
in the hopes that St. Nicholas
soon would be there.

The children were nestled all snug in their beds
with Elf Pets that cuddled near each of their heads.
And in my red suit complete with my cap,
I waited up **late**, never taking a nap.

Then out on the lawn there arose such a clatter,
I sprang from my shelf to see what was the matter.
Away to the window, I flew like a flash,
and hoped it was Santa arriving at last!

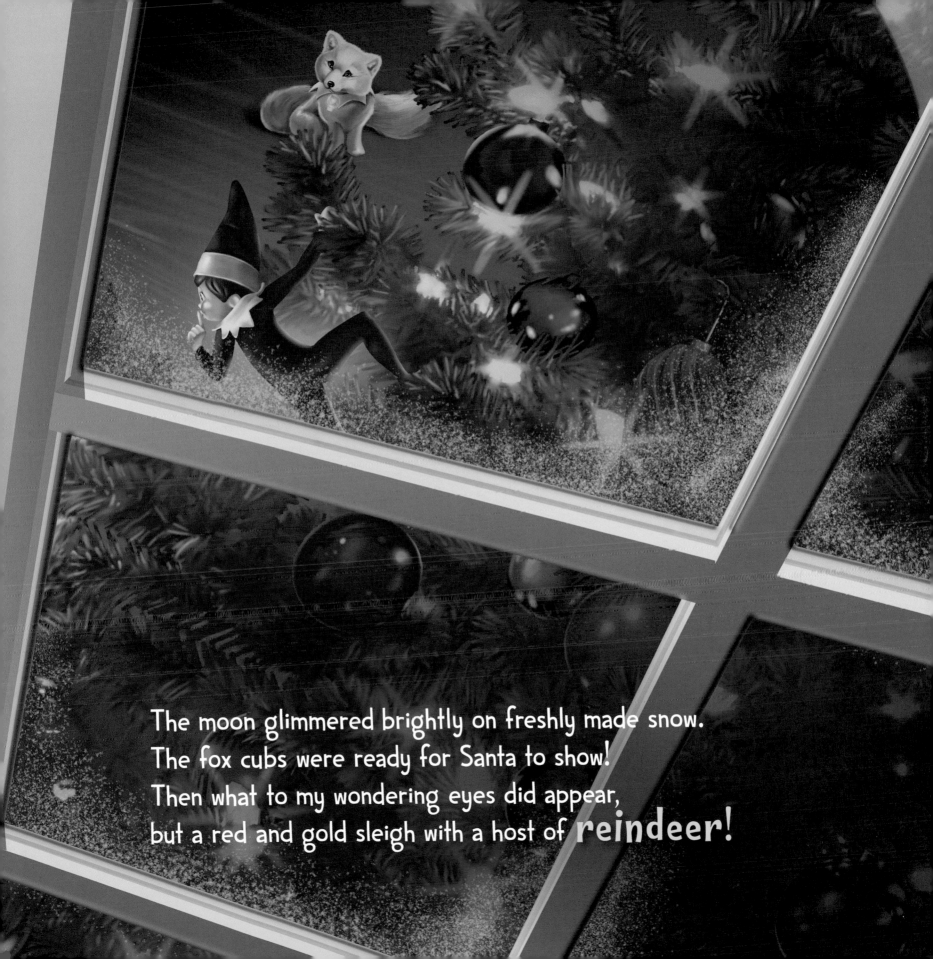

The moon glimmered brightly on freshly made snow.
The fox cubs were ready for Santa to show!
Then what to my wondering eyes did appear,
but a red and gold sleigh with a host of **reindeer!**

The **lively** old driver, so nimble and quick,
could be no one other than dear old St. Nick.
All of the reindeer together played games,
then Santa stood tall and called each by their names.

Now Dasher, now Dancer,
now Prancer, and Vixen;
on Comet, on Cupid,
on Donner, and Blitzen!
Go Husky! Go Hoofer!
Go Mister Fuzzball!
Now dash away, dash away,
dash away all!

The northern lights danced in the cold winter sky
as spirit swirled 'round helping reindeer fly high.
My house was in **mayhem** but what could I do?
The sleigh had arrived with St. Nicholas, too!

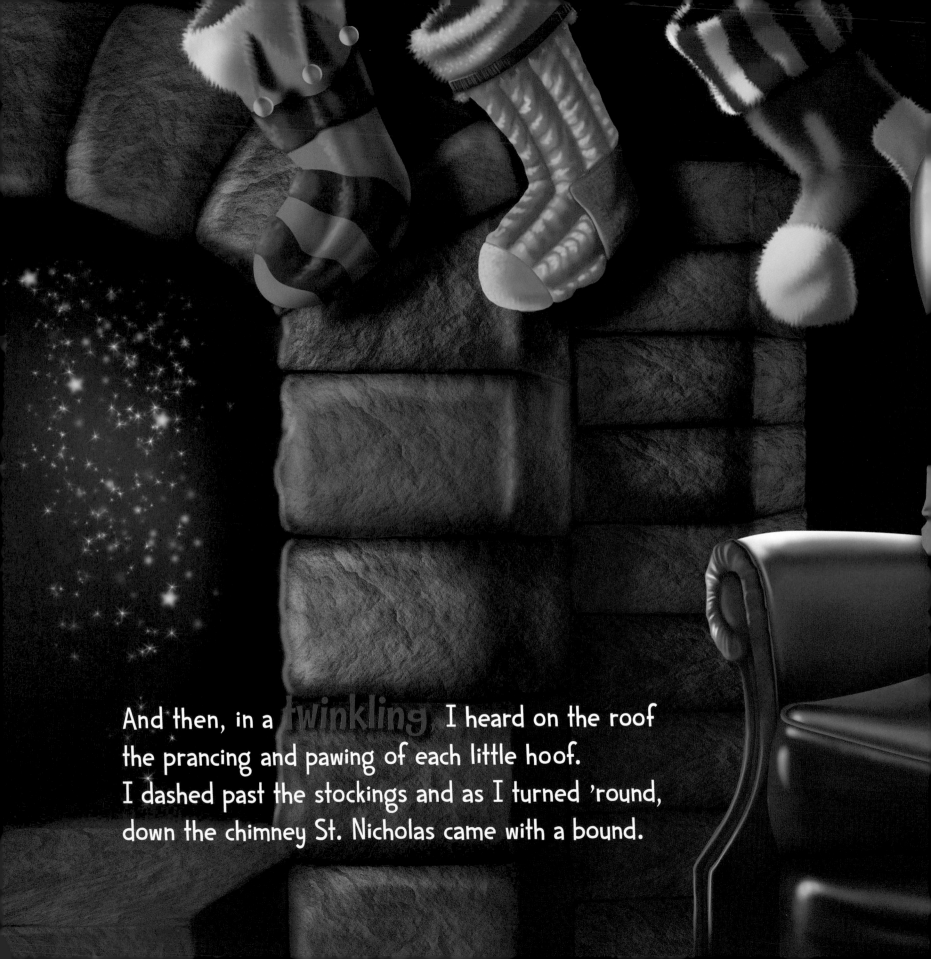

And then, in a twinkling, I heard on the roof
the prancing and pawing of each little hoof.
I dashed past the stockings and as I turned 'round,
down the chimney St. Nicholas came with a bound.

He was dressed all in fur from his head to his foot,
and his clothes were all tarnished with ashes and soot.
In the bundle of **toys** he had flung on his back,
some brightly wrapped presents spilled out of his pack.

His eyes—how they twinkled! His dimples—how **merry!**
His cheeks were like roses, his nose like a cherry.
He searched 'round the room, every garland and bow,
while smoothing his beard which was white as the snow.

He nibbled on **treats** and read letters beneath
the glow of the lights from our tree and our wreath.
When finally he spied me, his jolly round belly
shook when he laughed like a bowl full of jelly.

He was chubby and plump, like a merry old **elf**,
and I laughed when he saw me, in spite of myself.

With a **wink** of his eye and a twist of his head,
I knew that this Christmas was nothing to dread.

With a **snap** of his fingers, we both went to work.
When the stockings were filled, he turned with a jerk.
And laying his finger aside of his nose
then giving a nod, up the chimney we rose.

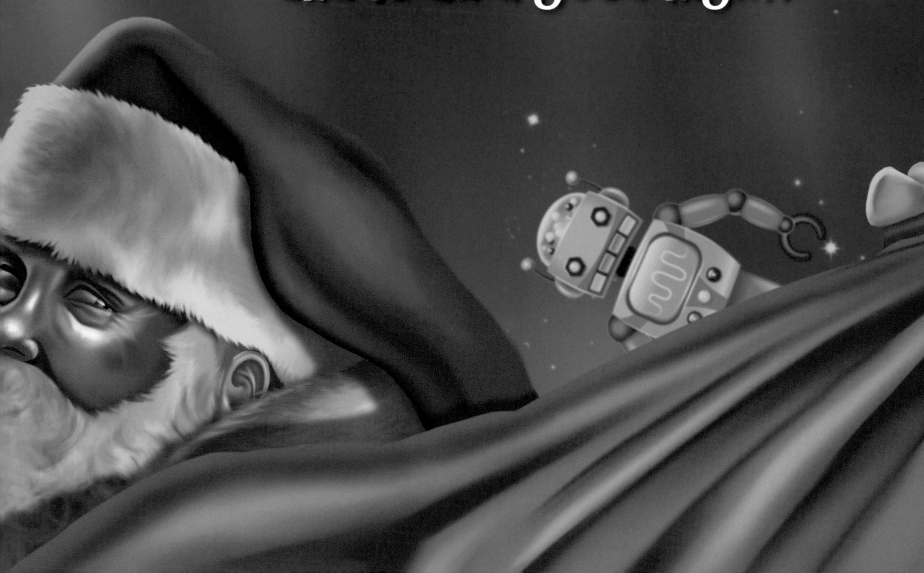

He sprang to his sleigh, and then signaled his team
and away we all flew like a magical dream.
And I heard him exclaim as we drove out of sight,

"Merry Christmas to all,
and to all a good night!"